Tilt - A - Whirl
on the Farm

poems by

Cele Bona

Finishing Line Press
Georgetown, Kentucky

Tilt - A - Whirl
on the Farm

For

my husband, Chuck, for his belief in my art

my children for enriching my life and not minding the clack

of my typewriter in the night long ago

poet Bruce Guernsey and friend Kathy Blair for helping birth this book

all my women friends, my village of support, creativity and laughter

ACKNOWLEDGMENTS

"Grandma Chased by a Bear," formerly, "Perception," appeared in *The Prairie Light Review*.
"Holding the Moon Between My Legs," First Place Jo-Ann Hirshfield Memorial Award, 2013.
"in the blank time," Second Place Jo-Ann Hirshfield Memorial Award, 2014.

Publisher: Leah Maines
Editor: Christen Kincaid
Cover Art: Nancy Saul
Author Photo: Shelly Asmussen
Cover Design: Elizabeth Maines McCleavy

Printed in the USA on acid-free paper.
Order online: www.finishinglinepress.com
                also available on amazon.com

Author inquiries and mail orders:
Finishing Line Press
P. O. Box 1626
Georgetown, Kentucky 40324
U. S. A.

Table of Contents

Holding the Moon Between My Legs

If I had obeyed I would have stayed
    in the hot farmhouse bedroom. I would not
have stepped out onto the moonlit porch,
    closing the screen without a sound.

If I had obeyed and followed the dictum:
    Do not go out alone at night, I would not
have walked barefoot—15—the dirt road to the pond
    a full moon flooding my long white nightgown.

I would not have seen the water black, glimmering,
    a streak of milk on top. I would not
have hung my gown on the branch of the weeping willow
    where it shimmered like my grandmother's ghost, she

who had patterned and cut and sewed the cotton plisse
    to just my size from three hundred miles away. Dead now,
was it she who smoothed my hair back
    and braided it loosely?

If I had kept the promise never to swim alone, I would not
    have climbed naked up the willow and out on its fattest limb
suspended over water. I would not have dived—virgin white
    skin—into that liquid night full

of frogs and fish and weeds and let everything touch,
    brush, titillate me. Under into depths, up into moonlight,
cool water soothing my hot body, tickling my tummy,
    kissing my tiny breasts, undoing my hair. I would not

have swum to exhaustion, rolled on my back, seen the moon
    shine my belly. I might not have grabbed
the full round moon between my legs and floated
    and come unknowing, ebullient, laughing out loud.

If I had not gone alone into the night, I might not
  have slept in the soft dust of the road,
not woken to birdsong at first light, doves cooing,
  swallows over the pond, redwing blackbirds commanding

the reeds. Wrens, goldfinch. A few butterflies nearby in the weeds.
  Cows bellowing in the back pasture, aching to be milked.
I might not have slipped back into the house
  unnoticed by all but the natural world.

Cleopatra in Her Garden

A bit like sex this picking tomatoes in October,
thought Cleopatra. The cold wind bit at her
breasts unharnessed beneath the plaid flannel
shirt. Slant sun fell warm as Anthony's kiss

on her bare neck. She popped a small
tomato still cool from the night into
her mouth, then reached for another. Sweet,
by the gods, sweet. This, against the pungent smell

of vine and fruit and earth climbing
her ankles, calves, thighs, made her rise
and ask, *Where is that man today? Without a war to plan
he grows melancholy and scorns my garden*

*and me perhaps. Surely this is a place
to love in.* She kicked at the soft mulch and laughed.
Lay her body down beneath the plants,
inhaled and slept. He would come by noon.

Evodia and the Snow Goose

That morning,
milking Evodia in her end stall,
the barn
exquisite with its limed white
aisles swept clean, the squirt, squirt
of milk hitting pails,
the Great Silence we kept
from evening prayers to breakfast,
hung in the air.

We eight women, all aspirants
to holiness, hand-milked the cows at dawn.
There was the slurp of silage, the drip
of udder cloths wrung out over pails
of disinfecting water, the sound of stantions
jangling, tails slapping.

Evodia's udder was warm, yielding.
She stood in her place eating
hay. As I pulled, her milk steamed
into the gleaming bucket.
Morning bloomed beyond the open door.

In the east, something backlit was flying
toward the barn.
A white snow goose swooped
inside, landed beside my milking stool
and gazed into my eyes. Then,

strutting up the aisle, she paused
beside each of my fellow seekers.
Vows silenced my voice. I could not
shout, *Look, look what we've been sent.
A gift.*

Parading back down the aisle, she
again held my eyes—
then flew off,
a lone speck in the morning sky.

When Uncle John Comes Over

From my bed I hear where he is
stomping the snow with black boots

now in the coop enraging
the hens, stealing warm eggs

singing up the back stairs
shouting us awake, cracking

an egg on the sink, leaning back,
way back, opening his mouth wide,

egg an arm's length above his head,
thumbs through the cracked

shell, gold yolk dropping on
a clear chain down his throat, sun

disappearing into night. He roars
and shudders. Then the whiskey

gloriously poured from the same height,
an amber stream of flame igniting

his feet, making him dance and shout—*the fire*
the fire has gone to my feet, is cooking

the eggs—He grabs my quilt, swings me up,
Please, my sweet, help your old uncle

put out the fire that's dancing the eggs,
cooking his feet, your cover to smother

the flames. He is big. I am small. He is fat.
I am thin. His back is the horse I ride.

playing hooky

like a fox she flew
across the field

lunch in a red kerchief
tied to a stick
set like a flag on her shoulder

allowed to stay home from school by her mother
who herself needed great gulps of sun and air
she galloped off and around her world

through the sumac to Kraut's farm
cold water from the spring house
on to the Outer Belt Line—
balanced on rails—listened for trains

hopped from mound to mound of dry grass
in the shallow swamp and when the sun went
straight up—ate a cold pork chop and carrots
in the woods by the creek

rolled down Johnson's hill
climbed apple trees in a left-over orchard
sweet with knowing her brothers and friends
were hitched to desks

at sundown she hiked up—down—up
clods of newly ploughed earth
toward the enclosed comfort
of kitchen, dinner, mother and the others

a gift seeded forever in her bones

Grandma Chased by a Bear

I rest my fingers on the dusty screen,
look out. Grandma chased by a bear,
she told me that

story. She was little,
running under pine trees
in the North Woods. She tore

her yellow pinafore on
thorns and was punished
for the tear, sent

to the hay mow for supper.
My old grandmother who
smelled like a rusty pump

pinned that story into
the hem of my green
skirt one October night.

I saw her frightened face,
her small feet flying over
brown pine needles to her aunt

who shook her, told her
not to make up stories.
Always before, seeing the

pins marching between her lips,
the steely hairs growing on her chin,
I thought she was always old.

No Peas Please

No peas, please.
Oh yes.
No. I won't eat peas.

So, sit there then
young lady till you do.

Past dishes
past the kitchen floor swept
past Fibber McGee

I sit. Past
the house going dark
except this room.

Everyone in bed.
Just me and the peas
and one chandelier still up.

I sing to myself
to bite back.
I'm not afraid of night.

The dog down on the landing
snorts in her sleep, the furnace
clunks. Father's voice distant

says, *Oh Christ.*
I gentle the plate aside;
put my head on my arms.

Past midnight mother
steals into the kitchen
and removes the plate.

Oh, for God's sake go to bed then.
Even in my grogginess
I hear the anger gone.

In the morning, I see the peas
in the garbage. No one
mentions them.

tomato revelation

flat on our bellies
we crawl through clover

slip
into his garden
steal
4 red tomatoes

eat them
with snitched salt
in the cool
of the culvert

they taste of sun

safe on the road
we run
the boys faster

big shoes
appear
beside my bare feet

he is laughing
my grandfather
he does not say
you're going to get it
little lady

I stop—
sit on a rock
and watch
him chase
my brothers
around the curve

heat hums in my ears
what's going on
here I ask the grass

The Summer She Was Four

Do not
pop
tar bubbles

when you walk
up the road
from the beach.

Sand, water, dust,
the gravel road,
travel beneath her skin.

At lunch I call,
get hot silence
outside the screen.

On a hill where
the road falls to
water, she

sits on little
pink heels
popping tar,

obeying
I guess
herself.

You have tar on your
swimsuit, it will
never come out.

Her eyes lifting
are sky, trees,
fish, lake.

Annie's Ice Cream Parlor

Cruising
down an ice
cream cone
after the
movies, a
little girl with
braids is
dismayed

> her chair
> all by
> itself
> slips
> out from under her
> bottom

from the floor
she cocks her
head at it
and you can
see she is wondering
how it did such
mischief so fast.

The Story Told in the Shop

The story told in the shop was that my father
gave blood right from his body to hers;
he lay down on a gurney next to my mother and
they hooked him up to her and that was what
saved her life.

He was a hero
to the customers, the vendors, his brothers,
sons, everyone who worked with him
in the butcher shop. They salted him with honor.

I was nine years old and to me my father
seemed as he always had—blunt
and loud. His body was loud. I wanted
to ask where they buried the baby? But
was afraid. No one said.

When my mother came home
unblooming, her hands old,
I wanted to give her something to fatten
her up and breathe shine onto her face.

I thought it was my mother who was brave
to let us see her plucked and shorn.
When we met at the door we fell
into each other's arms and held on.
No one could pull us apart.

1949

I am fourteen, riding to school in the cab
of my father's truck.
Tears and snot run down my face and off
my chin. My embroidered handkerchief
and sleeves are used up. The air
is clouded with smoke.

No, you won't. Never again—

He slows the truck, pulls to the curb
and jams the brake; my books spill
to the dirty floor. He takes his cigar
from his mouth, spits
out his window—
*Then your dog will be dead
when you get home from school.*

I open the door,
slide off the torn green leather seat straight
down to the street, not using the running
board—
some voice speaks for me—
Then she'll be dead.

I slam the door. The truck roars away.

Collected Stories with Footnotes

If you are not an abused little girl
in a big person's body
you might feel soiled, like a dirty handkerchief,
if you read this poem or
you might go dead calm, leave your body
at the table like when your best girlfriend's father
slipped his hand way up high between your thighs.
It was her tenth and golden birthday party
and you threw up and cried and your mom
had to come and get you early before the games. But you
don't remember why, so perhaps you should stop reading now.
You might get seasick like after the coach cornered you
in the sailboat cabin, screwed you and threatened
to spread a rumor you gave him blow jobs after gym
and he might scar your face too. Then he yelled up to the others
to mind the sheets. No, don't read this if you were never thrown
into this dumpster. If you didn't feel confused as a toddler
when your grandfather set you on his lap,
wrapped your legs around his waist and bounced you up and down
and a funny look came on his face and he kind of drooled
but not really and you giggled and laughed and screamed to be let go
but he held you tight against himself and sometimes
when your mother heard the two of you so loud,
she came and snatched you away, then don't read this.
 If you never went for a walk with your big sister
on a Saturday afternoon to the city park and you two never passed
all those pasty men with their car doors open wide, sitting sideways
on the seats, feet on the curb, their pants unzipped, calling out,
"Hi there, Sweeties," then don't read this.
If your own father never fucked you, just quit now.

Stage Directions
[Depression is played by Dark Beast]

January, dusk, daylight running down the gutter—

Your Dark Beast lies unseen
beside the warming fire,
his snout rests on your feet—
deep in a book, you do not feel the weight.

When you rise and head to the kitchen
for water—your throat feels parched, maybe you are
coming down with something—
he stalks and attacks;
strips muscles and tendons from neck and shoulders,
devours your bowels, chews daintily
on knees and feet—your little hands flap about,
the last to give up.
Blood pools on the stain resistant carpet.

Your voice—everyone said it was beautiful,
you should do something with it, will never be heard.

The Dark Beast Tries a Con

Beyond the bedroom window
the morning wears horizontal stripes—

a thin line of steel gray water
a band of silver clouds

a fat swatch of blue sky.

He is standing beside
the bed when I wake, holding out

a white silk robe for me to wear
down to breakfast.

Remember, you've been dismissed,
I chide as I

scoot out
the other side and jump

into red scuffs.
In my pocket little

legal pills.
On shore a single Ash

throws gold coins
up into the air.

When a Flower Is Not

January. These daisies woo
me. Evanescence captured
in green buckets
near cash registers.
Yet, they won't last. A father's
voice. *At this latitude*
winter lasts longer than summer.

White petal shy upon white
petal centered with yellow,
a merry-go-round of innocence
I dare not think.

Beyond the automatic glass
doors I smell cloudy
water, curled petals turned dark,
sharp dry stem through the heart.

The Body Politic

How many times did she go to sleep at night
sweetly softly deeply her gown riding up
one foot out of the covers—the breath going in
the breath going out—
when the army of men with daggers
entered her body under cover of darkness.

Sometimes there were random but precise
stabbings—the right knee, left big toe, a line
of hits from hip to heel.
Like pain on a pilgrimage.

There was the huge stone thrown over the wall
onto her chest. The poison inhaled. The ground war
with roots, steps, pillars: catapulting her forward,
flat, sometimes broken. Cut glass in her lunch.

How to be prepared? Each attack a betrayal
slung out of a sailing blue sky. How
could she be ready? Not trained as a warrior
she arose each day with arms outspread
expecting blessings.

Tree Life

The textures talked
As the sun curved down.
Rough ridges and hidden crevices
Told of the flesh they had touched.

When he was seven with his sneakers wedged in my crotch,
He was king
King of the world.
My self and the wind appointed him to rule.

Seventeen, the boy and girl
Leaned against my spring trunk.
Love oozed sweet and wild,
Sun-kissed in leaf shadows.

Twenty-four, alone,
Forehead pressed to the bark
Making marks like fire against the tears
His father seeking the earth, dead like my leaves.

Thirty-two to fifty-six, concrete claimed him
Smooth streets and suburban lawns.
He rode on wheels to fortune
I ached for his touch.

Sixty-five, his foot sound travelled, touched my roots.
Hoisted high, wedged, the boy squealed,
"I like it here, Grandfather. I feel like a king."
"I know," He replied, and lightly picked at my bark.

First Warm Day

After winter, the disabled
boy has become a young man.
He waves from his special
bike. His father rakes leaves
from under bushes.

The orange cat, in a pool
of sunlight, sleeps.

A new neighbor,
till now unseen, straps
his snowmobile to its trailer,
tows it into the third bay.
His boat, sleek as a thoroughbred,
stomps its hooves in the driveway.

The woman next door says she got
so hot on her walk she took off
her jacket. Tied it around her waist.
Her dog Bauer slips his leash and leaps
through an open car window.
Sitting straight up in the driver's seat
he's smiling—
he smiles a lot.

Everybody's out;
we're all out
walking, talking, washing cars,
digging in the dirt, pulling
big flower pots out of our garages;
and
like the maple, magnolia,
crocus, even our sturdy yew,
we are all turning our faces
up toward the sun.

In April

The tin of ski wax on the kitchen counter. The young mother on
the greeting card reading to her daughter wears a sheer dust cap.
Frogs sing day and night. They trick the man into naps, nostalgia,
languid sex. He thinks it a late summer evening day after day.
Then the sun rises and smacks his eyes a good one. The whole
county stops to listen. School buses too. Summer peck-pecks its
way up toward him like a new chick. This bird and that appear—
cardinal, goldfinch, red-winged blackbird, a single blue heron.
Long skis fall over in the night. "You have a lot of little coves,"
he tells his wife. He is trying to get back into his body, circling
around it. A slender pocket knife breathes with his thigh. Left for
repairs last fall, the lawn mower is lost.

in the blank time

when days
arrive
as snow

without sky
sun
stars

after a child
dies

a white
tomb builds
piece by geometric

piece   mute as
ice you let it
climb your body

as it would
a fence

inside grief
you turn and turn

rump up   knees
tucked   thumb in your
mouth searching

for a place
on your tongue
not sore

Cameo

As if on a leash suddenly shortened
I am pulled
back to the high bedroom dresser
where acorns in their newborn caps
rest in a china tea strainer.
Tiny roses, wine and pink, run around its sides,
the rim edged in gold.

These are acorns from the tree
that shades our babies' graves—
seeds that fell too soon
collected before they could root.

All Along the Back Fence

Lilacs, when you bloom
in May, another's face
will be in the kitchen window,
another's hands will carry
you into each room. On Mother's
Day when you unbind your beauty
all along the back fence another
child's candles will be on the cake.

The people on the patio
will not have just
come back from the lake.
They will sit in lawn chairs perhaps drinking
martinis straight up. Your green leaves
form a thick screen. A toddler
jumps off a boulder at the edge
of the lawn where our old
dog sleeps.

Lilacs, I carry you
and your scent on my tongue. On
Mother's Day I will open my arms 100
feet wide and gather you into my body
as always, Your cool blossoms brush
my breasts, put luscious, sexual love
in all my rooms. We are married, you
and I, animal and vegetable.
I sink my roots beside yours;
we are entwined together and apart.

Outrigger

The day my mother has her stroke
I am at the shore—I walk
into the water and begin to shake,
no one
can still or warm me.

My toddlers play in the sand. They dig
with yellow shovels and make castles
using their blue plastic buckets; build walls
against attack. They call out, "Look, Mommy.
Look what we made. Aren't they beautiful? Look."

I hear them and do not hear them. I go farther out—

"Look Mommy, look. Mommy look
what we made."

Don't go away now,
I have little children you love little children
you like to play with them remember?
I'm teaching
them to swim, you taught me to swim so I wouldn't drown.

Someone guides me back.
The children clap and shout, "Look Mommy—look"
The castles are perfect.
"How wonderful," I say.

The tide moves in, walls, castles, small stone
people
wash away.

Changing Places

Mother, go
to your room
at once
and find your
brain intact!
You must
remember where
you put it.
Just think.
You had it
only yesterday
right here in
the front hall—
remember how
we laughed?

Choosing a Nursing Home

The sturdy brick,
shining floors
aren't the only thing.

You must walk
unannounced
into the farthest

reaches; peer into
faint cracks
down which your tiny

mother can fall;
look at contorted
bodies wrapped around

wheelchairs and
sheets, smell the
smells that

cling
and decide what
tariff you too
can bear.

Later On

When she was 15,
a virgin and pure,
she didn't expect
at 60
to be taken
by slim, dark-haired boys
of 18.
It was a surprise.
Curious, she opened
an investigation,
volunteered in old folks' homes
and found her feelings
had been felt
before. Old eyes lifted,
brightened, remembering,
as she chatted, played cards,
Tuesday mornings.

Looking Ahead

The death
I wish
is of flowers

shriveling
becoming
seeds

disappearing among
dry stems, decaying
leaves

preparing
to live
again

sexy
soft moist petals
arranged.

gravity speaks through our feet

sheltered in time
we live   stars
realign like people in pews
asked to move over
let one more in
one more   in time

spinning around in
our space
we pass the sun
dance out   gravity
speaks through our
feet   gather
in   gather   in

gathered
by the light
of another   akin
opposed or simply
beside   we smash
clasp hands
hold on

Tilt-A-Whirl on the Farm

At noon I spy a spider in my spoon,
the quiet fan above goes round and round
and round. A tilt of silver casts a bug
on faces, cups and counter tops. *Oh look,*
my love, I put an arachnid on your nose.
Who knows what mischief yet awaits my hand?
Send in more spoons to make more spiders whirl
and dance, amuse and entertain our tribe
this hot and humid afternoon. While hay
lies cut and curing in the drying sun,
we've time to play and pray away the rain
that whines and bites the far horizon, rain
that will not feed but steal our grass from cow
and calf. It's time to eat your soup my loves,
to drown the spider in your spoon, eat
him whole and see him reappear. *Oh no*
sweet baby no, he's not alive; he's just
the fan going round and round and round.

Author's Note:

Before I could see over the top of the ironing board, my mother often set the iron aside and recited elocution pieces learned in high school. Up above her beautiful legs was her lovely voice, so early on, as I became enchanted by story, I became equally so by metaphor, meter, and rhyme. These were later echoed in years of dance lessons where my body sang to rhythm and sound—to the poetry of tap.

I grew up in the country outside Joliet, IL in a small house surrounded by open land, fields of corn and soy, a hill to sled down, ice to skate on, grandpa's garden to dig in, a tree of heaven to climb and read in, a rooster to wake me; my senses anchored and alert to the natural world. And then in high school, printed in large letters across the bulletin board of our homeroom was a quote from Keats' poem, "Endymion," reading, "A thing of beauty is a joy for ever." This was the first thing we saw every morning; we had studied the poem in class and intuitively I said yes to it. And so it began, my reading and writing of poetry. The exposure to good literature, especially poetry, that I received at St. Francis Academy, Joliet, IL, was very formative for me. It seeded my life as a poet and surely, if remotely, helped generate this book.

When I entered the University of Illinois Chicago, Program for Writers, I was in my forties and a wife, a mother of three, and a part-time reporter. For reasons unknown, I first registered in Fiction Writing, but was soon struggling. Then one day, looking down at my notebook, I saw its cover filled with poems, mine. I soon transferred to poetry, home at last, happy and productive. Since then, over the years I have published individual poems in journals, but not a collection such as this. But you don't publish your first chapbook at age 83 without a lot of support, and I want to thank those who helped me realize this book:

Thanks To:

Bruce Guernsey, editor emeritus of *The Spoon River Poetry Review,* and author of *FROM RAIN: Poems, 1970-2010,* for guiding my selection of thirty poems for this book out of the many written over a lifetime. A true mentor, he got *me* to select the poems.

Kathy Blair, expert file detective and tech whiz, without whom this collection would not even have begun. Kathy helped dig out misfiled poems, both electronic and paper. Without Kathy, many of my poems would still be lost.

Students Rose, Caroline, Katie, Annamarie, and Judy. Writer Margaret Peifer for pushing me to do a book. Poets Marilyn Taylor, Wisconsin Poet Laureate Emerita, Wendy Anderson, Ellen Savage, Gail Lukasik, and M.B. McLatchey. Also, poets Mary Wehner, Judith Barisonzi for helpful critiques. Poetry Square: Karen, Barb and Diane. Daniel Busch, M.D., practical advice. The Women's Exchange, Winnetka, IL, offering classes and support for women, where I taught for many years. Christi Mueller, Wendy Hamilton, technical help; Shelly Asmussen, author photo; Bonnie Dolter, addressing labels; Jen Garber, copy editing. Sisters of St. Francis, OSF, Joliet, IL, for planting those poetry seeds during high school. My mother, Anna Briick, for reciting verse when I was small. My brothers for reading poems aloud to me from their college texts. Also, to Bauer and Hank, Kathy's dogs, who often kept us company as we worked.